SUPER TECH
BIG DATA

CLIVE GIFFORD • CHELEN ÉCIJA

Enslow
PUBLISHING

Published in 2026 by Enslow Publishing, LLC
2544 Clinton Street
Buffalo, NY 14224

First published in Great Britain in 2024 by Wayland

Editors: Elise Short, Jenni Lazell
Designer: Lisa Peacock

Picture credits:
Hudl 23b. NASA/Ames Research Center 27b/IPAC-Caltech 26t/Keplar Space Telescope 27t.
Shutterstock: Andrew Angelov 7b; Mikolaj Barbanell 22tl; Christiano Barni 23t; Rick Carey 15t; r.classen 6t; Evgeniyqw 26b; Fizkes 11b; GAS-photo 14t; IamDoctorEgg 18t; Kentoh 14b; Kitreel 19t; Jane McKinnon 4b;Nostagrams 18b; ProStockStudio 10t; The Image Party 7t; 13_Phunkod 5t; Wassenbergh 11t; Weidong 5b; Monika Wisniewska 6b; Debbie Wong 22tr.

Manufactured in the United States of America

CPSIA compliance information: Batch #CSENS26: For further information contact Enslow Publishing LLC, New York, New York at 1-800-398-2504.

Please visit our website, www.enslowpublishing.com.
For a free color catalog of all our high-quality books, call toll free 1-800-398-2504 or fax 1-877-980-4454.

Cataloging-in-Publication Data
Names: Gifford, Clive. | Écija, Chelen, illustrator.
Title: Big data / Clive Gifford, illustrations by Chelen Ecija.
Description: Buffalo, NY : Enslow Publishing, 2026. | Series: Super tech | Includes glossary and index.
Identifiers: ISBN 9781978545410 (pbk.) | ISBN 9781978545427 (library bound) | ISBN 9781978545434 (ebook)
Subjects: LCSH: Big data--Juvenile literature. | Machine learning--Juvenile literature.
Classification: LCC QA76.9.B45 G555 2026 | DDC 005.7--dc23

Find us on

CONTENTS

WHAT IS BIG DATA?

The world today is packed full of billions of computers, smartphones, and other digital devices. These generate information known as data. As the numbers of devices have boomed, so has the amount of data.

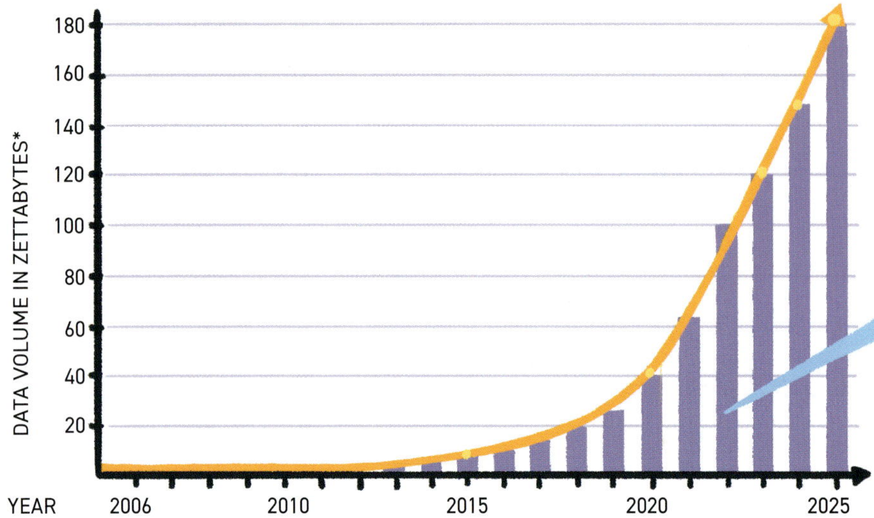

More data was produced each day in 2022 than existed in the entire world in 2008!

*1 ZETTABYTE =
1 BILLION TERABYTES

Big data is the name given to huge sets of varied data generated by large numbers of people and machines. Much of this data is gathered and stored, but it's not useful until it's sorted and analyzed by computers or people to discover links, patterns, and trends in the data that weren't known before.

Analysis of big data can advance knowledge or help companies find new ways to save money or sell more goods or services.

For example, big data analysis is predicting precisely where illegal tiger hunting is most likely to take place in India to help protect these endangered big cats.

WHAT SORTS OF DATA ARE GENERATED?

Social data is gathered by social media and streaming services. It may include your posts, messages, and status updates as well as what you like, share, and stream on networks.

Machine data is produced by a wide range of devices from simple parking sensors that can detect if a space is filled, to fitness trackers, smartphones, and space satellites orbiting Earth.

Transactional data is generated when you buy or use something including using an app to travel somewhere or enter a visitor attraction.

EVERYDAY DATA GATHERING

SMART SPEAKERS

These devices convert your spoken questions or requests into answers or actions. Your voice recordings and requests are just one form of data the speaker may collect. Others include your address book contacts, online searches you make, what apps you use, and other smart devices in the home.

BRUSH UP ON BIG DATA

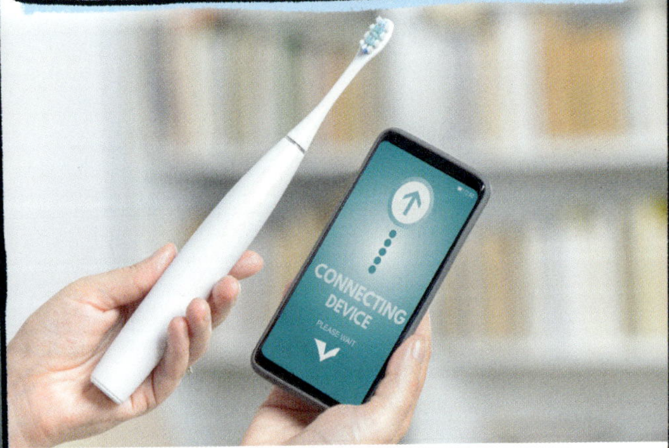

New, supersmart electric toothbrushes can connect to a user's smartphone using Bluetooth to send back data to an app. This analyzes the user's brushing movements and can point out areas that need a bit more brushing, or a change of toothbrush tip to tackle a particularly tough spot to reach.

SMART CARTS

Smart carts, like Amazon's Dash Cart and Kroger's KroGO, scan purchases automatically so customers don't have to stand in line at checkouts. Future smart carts may gather data on shoppers' behavior, such as at which shelves they linger most. This data may lead the store to change its layout or offer certain promotions to particular shoppers.

IMPROVING APPLIANCES

Some smart home appliances send back data to the companies who made them. The latest iRobot Roomba vacuum cleaners send back data from their cameras and other sensors. This is analyzed to give the robots a detailed map of the building and to help it recognize obstacles. Data about the robot's performance is also sent back and analyzed so the manufacturer can see how the robot is used by customers and where improvements could be made for future models.

A CLOSER LOOK AT:

THE INTERNET OF THINGS

Lots of objects and devices – from toasters to robotic vacuum cleaners – have computing technology inside and can connect to the internet. This can make them more useful, receive upgrades, communicate with people and other machines, and collect data. This network of machines is known as the Internet of Things.

A smart speaker's microphones send voice requests and questions over the internet to server computers that send answers back for the speaker to broadcast.

Smart ovens and dishwashers send data back to the manufacturer about their performance. By analyzing data from thousands of machines, the manufacturer can check on reliability.

A central heating system can be controlled over the internet by the owner even when they are not at home. Energy companies may analyze the system's data to get a better idea of home energy use and ways to promote energy efficiency.

The internet can also link to smart lights to turn them on and off.

A smart fridge monitors the food it contains and can suggest recipes, send alerts to the owner's smartphone, or reorder key items that are running out.

A smart door can alert the owner via their smartwatch or phone if it's not locked. It can also send video of visitors on the doorstep.

CHOOSING FOR YOU

ADS FOR YOU

Cookies are small data files kept about your visits and activity on websites. Some companies analyze cookies and other data such as your location or age to produce targeted ads for things they think you're likely to buy at certain times, such as around your birthday or before a holiday.

WHAT'S ON?

TV streaming services, such as Netflix, analyze what their customers watch, when and how. Did they race through a series or give up halfway through? Which parts did everyone rewatch? This data is used to recommend other shows but also informs companies about what new shows and movies they should make next.

MUSIC TO YOUR EARS

Music streaming services like Spotify and Deezer analyze customer data for patterns in behavior, such as skipping or replaying certain tracks by artists. Using programming rules called algorithms, the streaming service can automatically suggest particular songs or artists for each customer or make a mix or playlist likely to suit each listener.

A CLOSER LOOK AT:

THE FIVE Vs OF BIG DATA

Personalizing ads and streaming choices for you and everyone else requires lots of analysis of big data. This involves a lot of work behind the scenes due to how big, fast-growing, and varied big data can be. Five words, all beginning with the letter V, describe big data's key attributes.

The sheer **VOLUME** (amount) of data generated is HUGE. A lot is stored at data centers, which are big buildings containing thousands of server computers. Many centers can store more data than half a million personal computers added together!

A large data center can use enough electricity to power 80,000 homes.

VELOCITY is the high speed at which data is created and how quickly it moves. Many tasks from managing city traffic to making financial decisions in business may need data to flow almost instantly so decisions can be made fast.

Big data has **VARIETY**. It can include emails, photos, voice recordings, sales, and price data from cash registers, and machine data from cars and robots.

VERACITY asks: how accurate is the data? Some data may contain errors or gaps. This data needs to be "cleaned" by special programs or by people to be made useable and useful.

VALUE is about whether the data collected is useful. It can cost a lot of money to gather and store, so it needs to be helpful in some way. Questions typed into search engines, for example, are analyzed so the engine can speed up search results by preparing faster, ready-made answers.

BIG ISSUES, BIG DATA

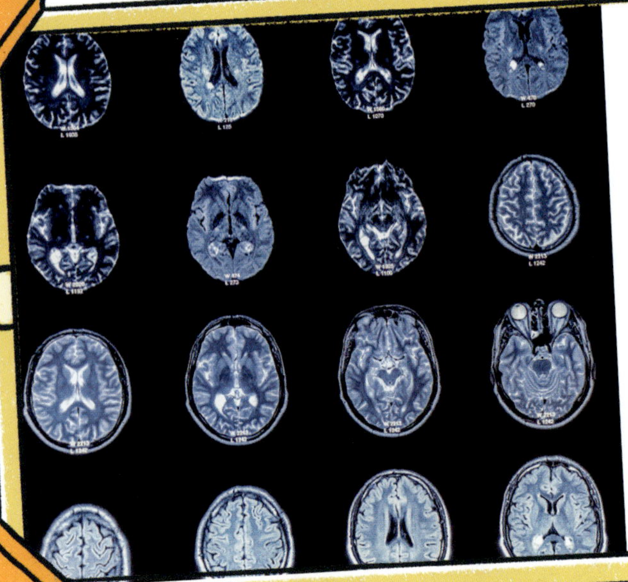

MEDICINE

Data-driven medicine is booming. Some medical facilities are scanning all their patient radiographs (X-ray images) so they can form a big dataset on computers that can be searched and analyzed. Researchers could use this to investigate links among various health problems and even identify possible future treatments or cures.

CRIMESTOPPERS

Some police forces use AI systems to delve deep into crime statistics and map their location. These systems identify crime hotspots and particular times when certain crimes are more likely to occur. Armed with this information, police can increase patrols in certain places or at certain times to stop or catch criminals.

SAVING TREES

The World Wildlife Fund and partners are using big data to stop the illegal cutting down of tropical trees and other protected species. The project analyzes vast numbers of records of timber shipments to identify illegal cargoes of protected trees and then lets local police and governments know.

WEATHER FORECASTING

Weather stations and orbiting satellites send large amounts of climate, temperature, wind, rain, and other weather data to meteorology centers. Many of these use powerful supercomputers to analyze the data in order to forecast what the weather will be like in the days ahead.

A CLOSER LOOK AT:

SUPERCOMPUTERS

Weather forecasting is just one of many applications that have so much data to handle they need particularly fast and powerful computers known as supercomputers. These machines are packed with not one but many central processing units (CPUs) – the brains of a computer.

One example of a supercomputer is the Frontier, which is one million times faster than a typical laptop computer.

CPUs are arranged in groups called nodes. A number of nodes may be fitted to a single circuit board, which is known as a blade.

The blades slot into racks inside cabinets. A supercomputer can consist of many cabinets and thousands of CPUs, giving them enormous computing power!

A regular computer with one CPU performs what's called serial processing, tackling one task at a time. But a supercomputer with lots of CPUs can break up big tasks into chunks and handle them all at the same time, speeding things up.

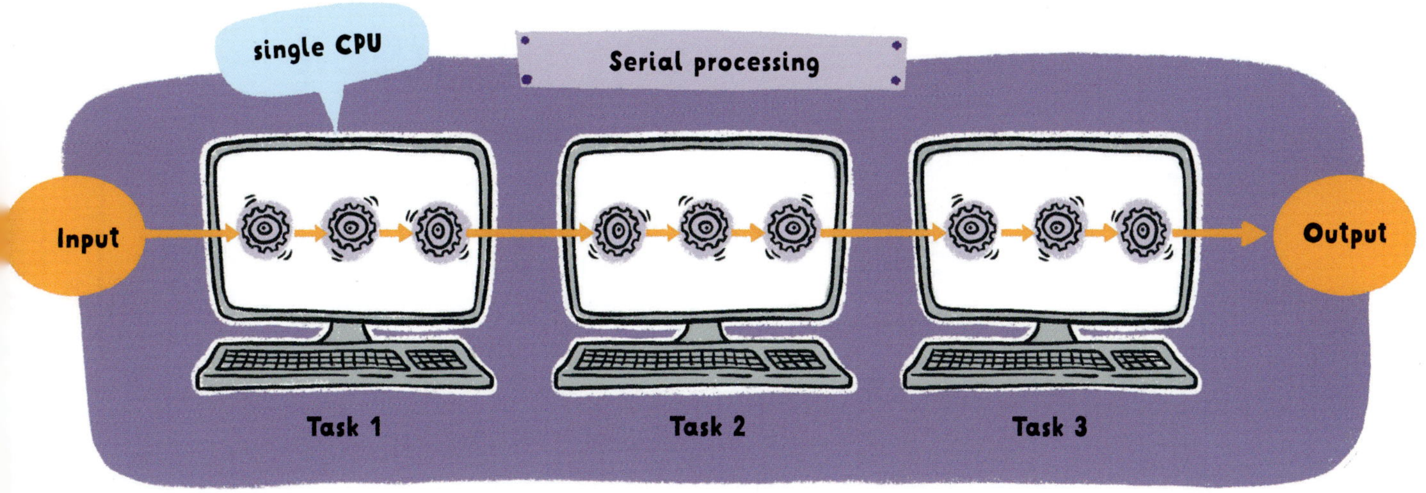

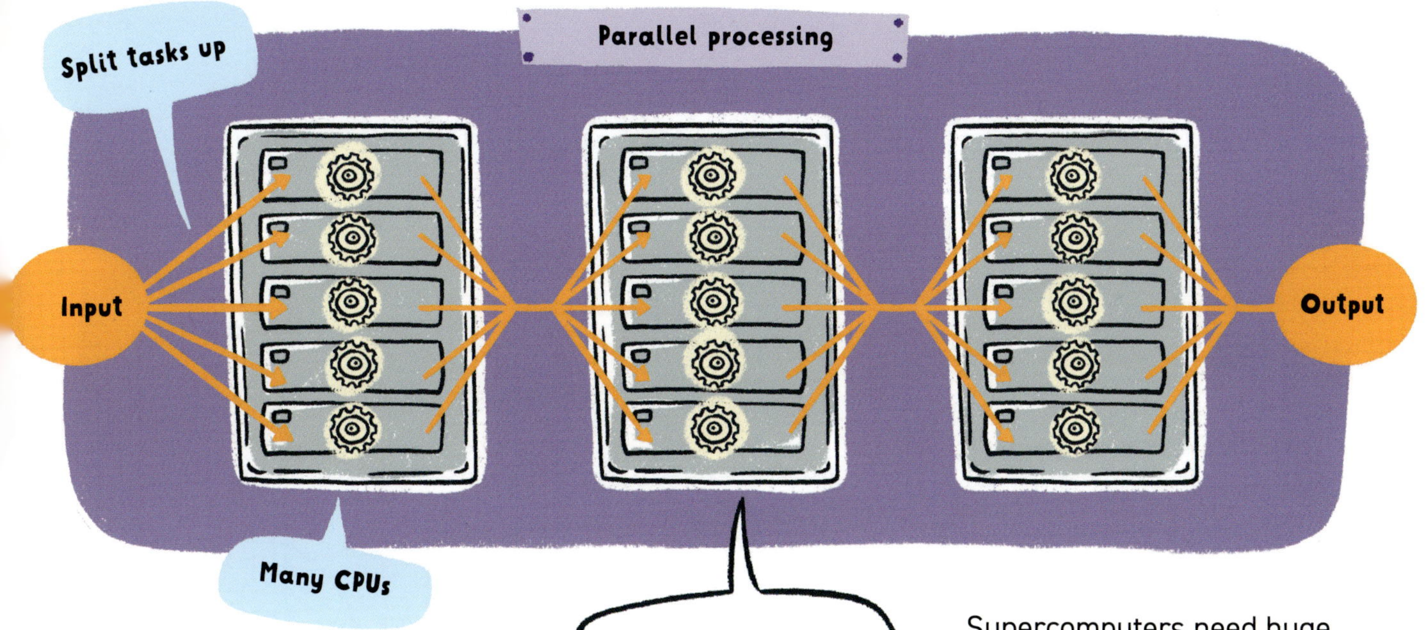

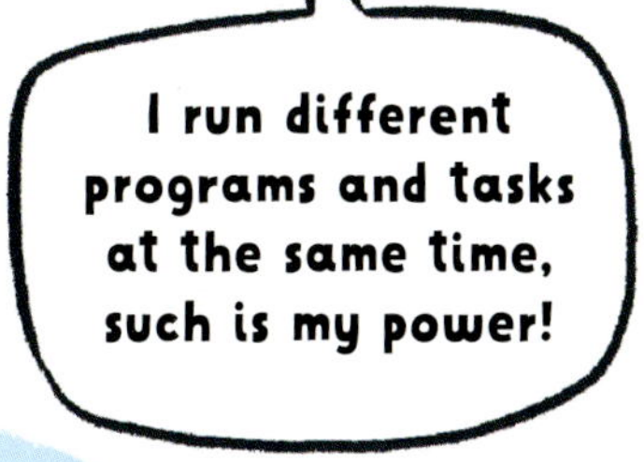

Supercomputers need huge amounts of memory to handle all the data they process. And they also consume a lot of electricity, both to run all their CPUs and to keep their processors cool.

This supercomputer has run a detailed simulation of how a tropical storm develops. The simulation is displayed on screen for scientists to investigate.

DATA ON THE MOVE

SHINKANSEN

Japan's high-speed rail network uses big data to predict customer numbers on future services. It also analyzes data to forecast the reliability of both its trains and track so it can fix problems before breakdowns occurs. As a result, the average train delay is under one minute. Brilliant!

TAXI!

Smartphone taxi apps store data on every trip their customers make, including the most common pick-up points and destinations. This data is analyzed so the taxi companies can predict what places will be busiest and to match drivers to customers as efficiently as possible.

SMART LENS

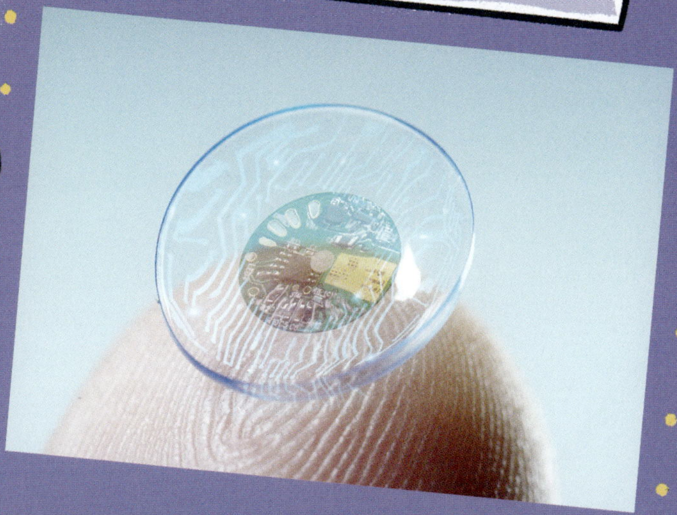

Companies and labs are attempting to develop smart contact lenses that display information in the corner of your field of vision. Future lenses may be 3D-printed and display traffic data, map directions or vital information about a task you are performing.

A CLOSER LOOK AT:

VIDEO ANALYTICS

Smart cities are analyzing big data to predict where traffic jams and congestion will occur at different times of the day. This data is used to alter route suggestions, road speeds, and traffic light timing to keep traffic moving. But it's not the only city data being looked at and acted upon.

Video footage of traffic is sent by radio signals to a traffic center's video analytics system. It uses AI to recognize different kinds of vehicles, the speed of traffic, and the length of traffic jams. Data fed into the predictive traffic system allows it to forecast where problems are most likely to occur in advance.

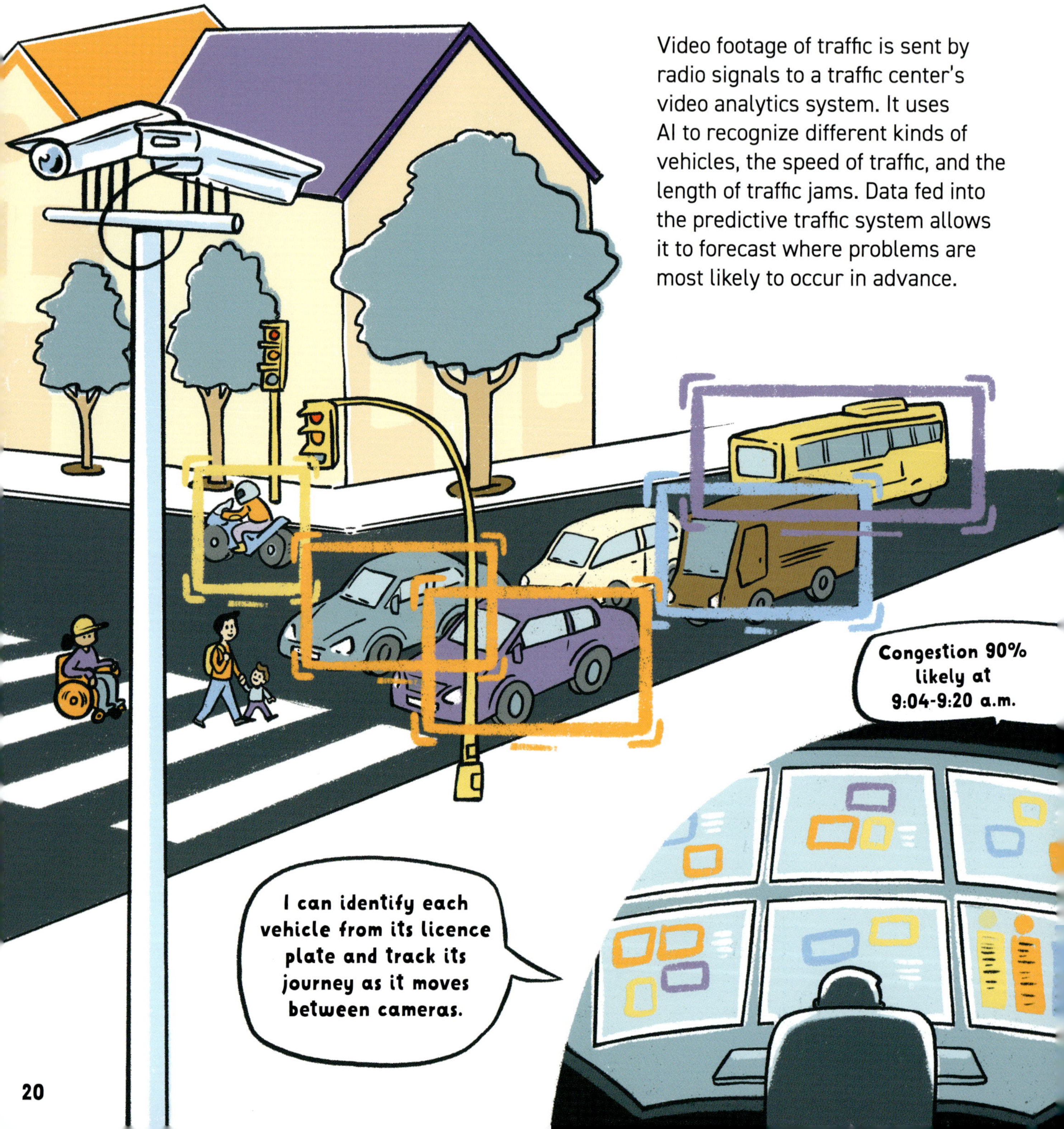

Environmental agencies may focus their studies on traffic hotspots to measure air pollution and to see its effects on nearby plant life.

Urban planners use video analytics to measure which are the busiest pedestrian areas at different times. Analysis can also reveal how people interact with the city's roads, crossings, and public spaces, and if there are any accessibility issues.

Planners may widen pavements or add benches or road crossings in places most used by people on foot.

They may even change the layout of the city by closing off some roads to motor vehicles or redirecting traffic away from the busiest areas.

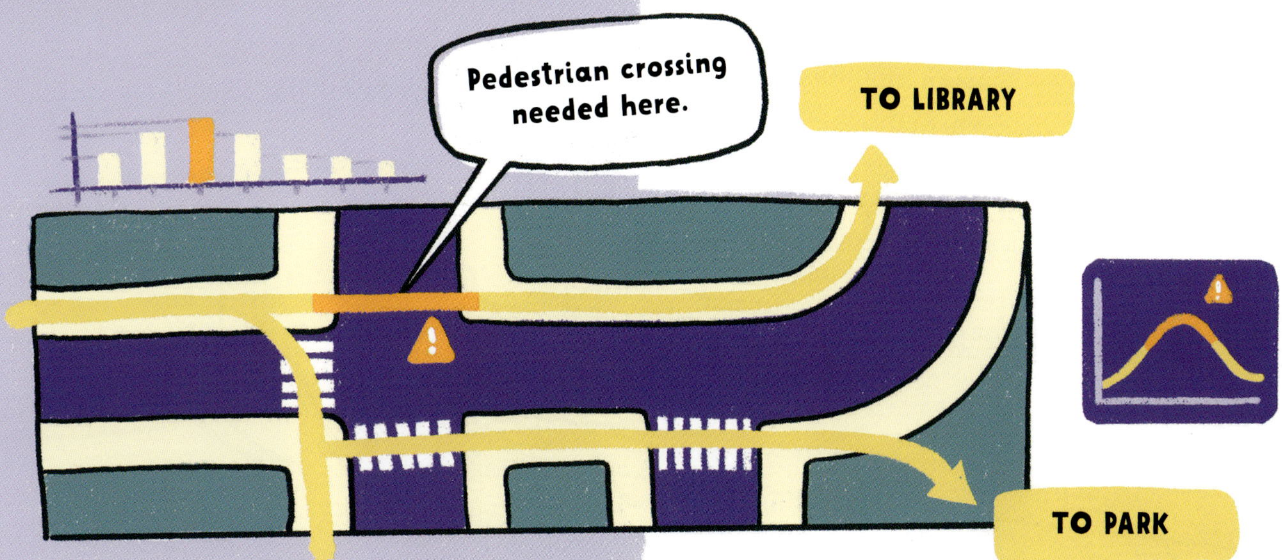

BIG DATA IN SPORTS

SCOUTING AND RECRUITMENT

Professional teams increasingly use big data analysis of players to identify the best new recruits. The Boston Red Sox baseball team built a computer database called Carmine to help identify talent based on data. It helped result in the Red Sox winning the World Series four times!

TRAINING DATA

Many athletes train wearing vests or harnesses containing sensors including GPS, oxygen monitors, and accelerometers, which measure changes in speed and direction. The data is analyzed to calculate the athlete's sharpness and fitness levels, if they've recovered from injury, and whether they're ready for the next competition or game.

DATA ON TRACK

Few sports generate as much data as Formula One. F1 cars contain over 300 sensors that send back gigabytes of data every lap on everything from air flow and cornering speed to tire wear and brake temperature. The data gives race engineers instant information to alter car settings or driver tactics.

HUDL SPORTSCODE

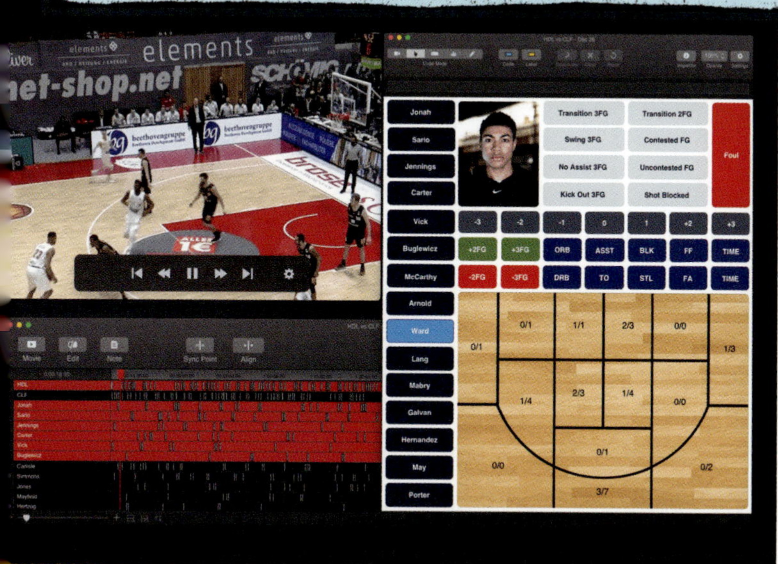

This tool captures video and data using special cameras from training or competitive sports games. They allow video analysts in many team sports to build up data sets on opponents' movement, passes, and plays. Coaches can use this data to pick their teams and tactics to outwit their opponents.

A CLOSER LOOK AT:

SPORTS STADIUMS

Modern sports stadiums use big data in their design and day-to-day operations. This can include the creation of a digital twin – a complete virtual stadium made of data and computer code. The twin can be used to monitor the flow of people inside the stadium and how all of its power, plumbing, and lighting systems are working.

A giant screen on each side of this cube displays game and player stats before, after, and during breaks in the game.

The fan's ticket on a smartphone is scanned and data on that fan, such as when they've arrived, is stored. This can be used to help plan when to open stadium facilities and to send messages to entice the fan to other games.

The in-game data is sent to the stadium's press box and TV studio. TV commentators may quote some of the data as statistics during the broadcast of the game.

A stadium app provides fans with extra data on the stadium and the day's game. It may allow fans to order food, drinks, and souvenirs without leaving their seat.

Analysts watch the game and log game data such as the number of short and long passes, fouls, and which parts of the field have seen the most action.

Coaches also review the game data afterwards to see how their team played.

DATA IN SPACE

VISUALIZING SPACE

Space telescopes collect lots and lots of data, which is beamed back to Earth by radio waves for storage and analysis. Sometimes, data from different probes or telescopes are merged together to form images. This NASA image of the Andromeda Galaxy is the result of merging data gathered by four different space probes.

ROCKETING SUCCESS

New spacecraft like SpaceX's *Dragon*, are tested extensively on the ground before they're risked in space. Hundreds of sensors fitted to test models collect data, which is then studied in great detail. It can reveal weaknesses or problems with parts, speeding up the time it takes to get the spacecraft just right.

PLANET HUNTER

Exoplanets are planets outside our solar system. But we didn't discover them until the 1990s. In 2017, analysis of big data held from the Kepler space telescope about one star system revealed a brand new planet (called Kepler-90i), about 1.4 times the size of Earth.

PLEIADES SUPERCOMPUTER

This powerful computer stores data from earlier NASA space missions. The computer's over 220,000 CPUs can turn some of the data into simulations so that scientists can investigate how stars form, or how gases leaving rocket engines might affect the flight of new spacecraft designs.

A CLOSER LOOK AT:

THE SQUARE KILOMETRE ARRAY

The Square Kilometre Array Observatory (SKAO) is the world's largest radio telescope. It features over 130,000 antennae which collect radio waves. They all work together as one HUGE telescope to produce VAST amounts of space data.

Large numbers of radio antennae, shaped like dishes or poles, are placed in parts of Australia and South Africa. In total, they cover an area of about 10.7 million square feet (1 million sq m).

The SKAO features enough fiber optic cable to circle the Earth twice!

Stars, galaxies, and black holes give off radio waves that travel through space. The antennae gather radio waves that reach Earth. They then send the waves via fiber optic cables to signal processors. These turn the waves into useful data.

The data is sent to the SKAO's two supercomputers for astronomers to investigate. These machines handle HUGE amounts of data. A regular desktop computer may have two terabytes of storage. The SKAO can produce 160 terabytes of data every second!

Supercomputer programs combine data from many antennae to produce radio wave images of space objects. Astronomers get to see distant objects in space for the first time or in far greater detail than before.

TECH TEST

See how many of these questions you can answer. Answers are on page 32.

1. What is the name of the data files kept about your activity and visits to websites?
a) Cookies
b) Nibbles
c) Biscuits

2. Which supercomputer is one million times faster than a regular laptop computer?
a) Pleiades
b) Taihu Light
c) Frontier

3. What is the name of the Japanese high speed train network that uses big data to predict reliability issues?
a) Shinkansen
b) Deezer
c) RapidÓ

4. Which baseball team built a database called Carmine that helped it win four World Series?
a) New York Yankees
b) Boston Red Sox
c) Toronto Blue Jays

5. How many terabytes of data can the Single Kilometre Array telescope produce each second?
a) 6
b) 36
c) 160

6. What word, beginning with the letter "V" describes the accuracy of data collected?
a) Volume
b) Veracity
c) Value

7. Which big organization uses the Pleiades supercomputer?
a) The United Nations
b) NASA
c) Tesla

8. What is the name of the data-gathering shopping cart used in some Amazon stores?
a) Dash Cart
b) KroGO
c) Speedkart

GLOSSARY

AI Short for artificial intelligence, the ability of machines to think and make decisions in similar ways to people.

antenna A pole or dish-shaped device which can receive and transmit radio waves.

CPU Short for central processing unit, this is usually a microprocessor that performs all the calculations in a computer and controls the computer's parts.

database An organized collection of information that allows data to be easily searched and retrieved.

GPS Short for global positioning system – an accurate navigation system based on satellites orbiting Earth.

Internet of Things (IoT) The connection to the internet of machines and devices with computing technology including cars and household appliances.

network Two or more computers or digital devices linked together in some way so that they can communicate with one another.

sensor A device that collects information about a machine or its surroundings.

server A computer used to hold and "serve" data to clients when they make a request for information.

simulation A program or system that mimics realistically another setting such as flying a plane or a phenomenon such as a storm forming.

spam Unasked for emails and messages copied and sent to large numbers of people often advertising something.

streaming A method of sending and receiving data, often sound or video, as a continuous flow from a server computer.

supercomputer A class of particularly large, fast, and powerful computer able to process huge programs and data tasks.

terabyte (TB) A measure of data storage equal to 1,000 gigabytes. A modern desktop computer may have one or two terabytes of storage.

FURTHER INFORMATION

BOOKS

Why AI?: All Your Questions About Artificial Intelligence Answered by a Computer Scientist by Dr. Dharini Balasubramaniam (Wayland, 2024)

Explore AI: Machine Learning by Sonya Newland (PowerKids Press, 2025)

ON THE WEB

https://royalsociety.org/topics-policy/projects/machine-learning/what-is-machine-learning-infographic/
A fascinating interactive webpage explaining how AI systems use big data to perform useful tasks.

https://codakid.com/blog/introduction-to-artificial-intelligence-for-kids/#Why_Kids_Should_Learn_About_AI
Explore more about AI here.

Every effort has been made by the Publishers to ensure that the websites in this book are suitable for children, that they are of the highest educational value, and that they contain no inappropriate or offensive material. However, because of the nature of the Internet, it is impossible to guarantee that the contents of these sites will not be altered. We strongly advise that internet access is supervised by a responsible adult.

INDEX

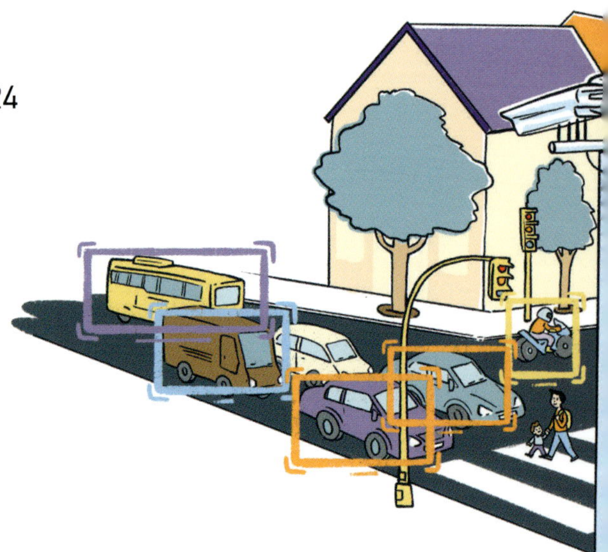

Answers
1.a, 2.c, 3.a, 4.b, 5.c, 6.b, 7.b, 8.a